Brazilian Jiu-Jitsu
Mental Drilling

S. G. Squires

ISBN: 1530268060
ISBN-13: 9781530268061

Legal Disclaimer

Table of Contents:

Acknowledgment…………………………………….9

Introduction……………………………………….11

Finding the Right Brazilian Jiu-Jitsu Academy…..13

Proper Mat Protocol……………………………15

Drilling…………………………………………16

Tapping Out……………………………………17

Give Yourself a Committed Timeline……………19

Belt Promotions……………………………….....21

Making the Most Out of Open Mat………………22

Escapes…………………………………………23

Taking Notes on Technique………………………25

How to Effectively Take Notes……………...……26

Honest Self Inventory……………………………29

Do Your Homework………………………….....31

Detail………………………………………..33

Be on the Attack…………………………………………34

Grip fighting……………………………………………..37

Pressure/Weight distribution……………………………39

Muscle Memory………………………………………….41

Mental Drilling…………………………………………...42

Having a Well-Rounded Game…………………………..43

The Advanced Game…………………………………….45

Having Multiple Routes…………………………………46

Connecting the Dots……………………………...………46

Sneaky Jiu-Jitsu…………………………………………48

The Guard………………………………………………...49

Passing Guard……………………………………………53

Openings for Guard Types……………………………...55

Guard Retention…………………………………………57

The Mount………………………………………………...61

The Back………………………………………………….63

Side Control……………………………………………….65

Competition Prep (dieting)………………………….....77

Starting from Your Feet………………………………...69

Transition Submission………………………....71

Using Submission as Controlling Position……….73

Reactionary Cues…………………………….....75

Pulling Sweep………………………………….77

Plateaus/Walls………………………………….78

Muscle Strength……………………………….....81

Fatigue………………………………………….84

Energy Conservation……………………….…....85

Going Light…………………………………….86

Injuries ………………………………………….87

Proper Protective Gear……………………….….91

Training While Injured…………………………....92

Strength Supplements……………………….…....95

Joint Supplements……..………………….…....96

The Blue Belt Relationship Counselor……….…...99

Acknowledgment

I want to first thank my beautiful wife for all the love and support that she gives me in achieving my jiu-jitsu goals. I want to also thank all my various BJJ instructors and team mates that have offered so much in my development. Special thank you to my sister for all her help. Most of all I want to thank my Father in Heaven and Jesus Christ for helping and blessing me in all my endeavors.

Introduction

The information in this book was written for the purpose of assisting you in your BJJ progression. The concepts and principles included herewith are proven to be effective at increasing retention level, overcoming plateaus, competition readiness, overall game development, and a whole lot more. Some sections of this book are specifically targeted for the beginners, while other sections supplement the more advanced practitioner. Ultimately, this book is designed to help you get the most out of your training, accelerating you to the next level in your jiu-jitsu journey.

Finding the Right Brazilian Jiu-Jitsu Academy

Key points in selecting the right BJJ academy:

- See what academies are local to home/work.

 The closer the academy, the more likely you will make it to class.

- Check online reviews.

What are people/students saying about this academy.

- Visit the academies' web sites.

 Specifically check for class schedule and instructor bio/info.

The next step would be to either call the academy to speak to the instructor, or just show up at a scheduled class time and ask to observe a class.

Questions to ask on phone, or at end of observed class:

- What is the class schedule?

- How do promotions work?
- Any restrictions on gi (uniform) types, or colors?
- Monthly cost/contracts? How many classes can you attend per week?
- Instructor's lineage?
- Any special attention, or classes for beginners?
- Does the head instructor teach the majority of classes, or do selected students?

In observing a class, look for the following qualities:

- Facility cleanliness
- Mat space
- Technique instruction is easy to understand.
- Instructor is tentative in assisting students to learn properly and safely.
- Students have good/helpful attitude.

Proper Mat Protocol

General:

- Always show respect to your professor/coach/master. Addressing your instructor with the proper title is a great way to show respect.
- In some academies students will bow before stepping on the mat.
- No shoes on the mat.
- Clean body and uniform
- Cut/manicured nails

Rolling:

- Tap hands before rolling.
- Focus on technique. Trying to plow through your training partners with brute strength will not allow you to learn proper technique, and you will often injure yourself and others. In other words, don't be a spazz.
- Be respectful when training with the opposite sex.
- Don't celebrate when you tap out training partners. Maintain a humble attitude toward fellow students.
- As with the last bullet point, be humble when you tap out. Displaying anger, or frustration toward fellow students is very disrespectful, and lacks sportsmanship.
- In some academies, it is more appropriate to allow upper belts to invite you to roll with them.
- Always thank your training partners for the roll.

Drilling

A big part of any Brazilian Jiu-Jitsu class is drilling technique.

First, your instructor will show you and narrate how to do a specific technique, such as, triangle from closed guard, x-pass to armbar, or butterfly sweep to mount. Pay close attention to all the details, so that you will drill the technique properly. Look for specific grip types, feet placement, posture, weight distribution, execution, etc.

After showing the technique a few times, the instructor will usually give opportunity for questions. If you have any questions regarding a specific technique, always ask. You could even request that your instructor show you the technique another time, so that you can commit it to memory for your drilling.

Now it is time to drill. Drilling commits what you are learning to muscle memory. If you feel that you are not performing the technique properly, ask your instructor to assist you. A good instructor will usually go around the mat helping individuals in their class correct any imperfections.

It is important to give yourself plenty of reps. This will greatly increase your retention level. Drill the technique until you develop the ability to reproduce the technique without conscious thought.

Also, focus on drilling the technique correctly. You may need to drill each step slowly before increasing your repetition speed to make sure that you are not missing any detail.

Tapping Out

Have the right attitude to tapping out:

Tapping out should be an excellent opportunity for you to recognize a hole in your jiu-jitsu game. Take special note as to what you need to improve on to prevent the same occurrence. For example, if you keep getting tapped out from an Americana from mount, your training focus should be on learning how to defend/counter the Americana from that position. You should take it back a layer further, and train on how you can prevent/escape the mount. If your training partner cannot get, or keep you in the mounted position, he/she will not be able to submit you from that position.

Unless you take an active approach to your learning by focusing on your weak areas, you will continue to relive the same scenario over and over again. Your regular training partners will be able to pick up on the gaps in your game, and capitalize on them for a quick submission.

Getting the tap:

When achieving a submission, carefully breakdown the steps in your mind as to what made the submission effective. Look for what was done correctly to accomplish the tap. Pinpoint specific details that could

have been included to sharpen/polish your execution of the technique, and include them in your training.

Take special note as to what defensive obstacles you were challenged with before getting the tap. Always look for ways to better counter your opponent's submission defense. Get help from your BJJ instructor in developing better offensive control and defensive grip breaking options. This will greatly increase the effectiveness of your submission attempts for getting the tap.

Give Yourself a Committed Timeline

For those that are starting out in BJJ, the first couple of months have the potential to be brutal. It is brutal in the fact that you will be spending a lot of time under the pressure and skill of higher ranking/more experienced students. Allow yourself time to adapt to the rigors of jiu-jitsu training. Humility is a key element to your success. There is also a period of time that you will not offer much offensively, or defensively, for that matter.

There is a definite learning curve with jiu-jitsu that may be compared to learning another language. If you commit your time to the mats though, it is inevitable that you will get better and enjoy success in your training. Don't be discouraged based on the first couple months, or so of getting smashed. We have all gone through it on some level. Give yourself a committed timeline.

For those who have been training for a while, having a committed timeline will help to get through periods in development that feel slow, or that may have stalled

altogether. There are inevitable plateaus and obstacles that all jiu-jitsu practitioners will be faced with in their development and training. This can only be overcome by giving the necessary diligence in training within a committed timeline.

There are many in the world that never reached the full potential of their development, only because they did not dedicate their time. This is sound advice for any life goals on, or off the mat.

Ultimately, the only way to reach your training goals is in dedicating your time. Look at all the great black belts of Brazilian Jiu-Jitsu; they are still actively competing and training. Those who truly commit themselves to the sport, reach far beyond what some may view as the end result (black belt). This is because the committed timeline never ends. It is a lifelong commitment.

Belt Promotions

Belt promotions may work differently depending on your instructor, or the academy you train in. If belt promotions are a concern, I would ask your instructor what he/she is looking for in that regard.

Focus should be on getting better every day, and not so much on the color of your belt. When you focus on progressing your skills to a certain level, promotions will inevitably come.

There are some fighting styles in the general martial art community that have a bad reputation for handing out undeserved express belt promotions. The high standards in Brazilian Jiu-Jitsu belt promotions though, are quite consistent, and rarely fall in this category. In other words, your belt will likely be well-deserved.

There are some academies that may have the potential to be strict with promotions. Don't let this be a discouragement to your progress. Again, focus should be on becoming better. I'm sure it's not a bad feeling, having the ability to handle some of the higher ranks on the mats, before getting a new belt.

Additionally, awarding stripes is another way that your jiu-jitsu instructor may gauge progress. Typically, students are awarded their 4th stripe before belt promotion is considered. Not all academies use the stripe system with their belt promotions.

Making the Most Out of Open Mat

Open mat is a dedicated time where students of all levels can casually enter the academy to participate in live sparring (rolling), as in contrast to a structured training class with instruction. Some academies generally welcome students from other BJJ academies/schools.

Although open mat is a period of time usually set apart for rolling, this is an excellent opportunity for BJJ

practitioners to work on specific areas of their game that need improvement. If there is a specific technique, or area you need help with, your training partners will typically help.

Have a goal in mind as to what you want to accomplish in your open mat training. Do not go with a casual mindset, or you will not take full advantage of this time.

Also, visit other academies in your area that offer open mat to neighboring BJJ schools. This will open the doors to new challenges in development.

Training with the same jiu-jitsu practitioners all the time will bring the same, or expected challenges that you are already familiar with. It is important to add new challenges in dealing with an unknown jiu-jitsu game, that a fresh training partner may present to you when sparring (rolling).

Escapes

Types of escapes:

In BJJ there are two types of escapes. These are positional escapes and submission escapes. It is important to have a number of varying options of escape for each position and submission. With this, you will have multiple pathways for technique, when any one of your routes of escape are obstructed.

Beginners:

For those beginning BJJ, learning escape techniques are not as exciting, or flashy as training submissions. The hard reality is that you will probably not have a lot of opportunity, or positioning that enables you to employ a submission. As a beginner, you will probably be spending most of your time in a situation that would necessitate an escape. For your jiu-jitsu to be enjoyable, it is necessary to know how to escape tough situations. The better you are at positional escapes, the less time you will be spending getting smashed under the pressure of your training partner's mount, side control, back control, knee on belly, etc.

Advanced:

For advanced players, there is usually a fundamental knowledge of positional and submission escapes. The focus at this level should be on closing any holes in your game. If you notice that you keep getting caught in certain positions, or submissions, you should dedicate your time and training on learning escape techniques specific to your weak areas.

Advanced practitioners should also focus on preventative measures in defense and guard retention that will reduce your exposure to potential offence.

Taking Notes on Technique

Without keeping a proper record, it could be difficult, to near impossible to remember a specific technique without constant review/drilling. In my own experience, even though I pay close attention to detail, and spend plenty of time drilling, there are many amazing and effective techniques that my jiu-jitsu instructor would teach that I could not remember. This is completely because I did not write down the specific detail of the move in note.

Taking notes will:

- Increase your retention level.
- Help you recognize holes in your game.
- Allow you to track your progress.
- Create a reference for review.

Review and Revisit:

Your records/notes will not be effective unless you review them. I recommend reviewing your notes at least once a week. Pull techniques from your notebook to add to your weekly personal drilling plan. Revisiting technique you have already learned will sharpen your execution of the move.

How to Effectively Take Notes

The purpose of this book is not just to give you useful information to supplement your jiu-jitsu game, but to show you how to effectively retain all that you learn.

First, write the name of the technique, and from what position. For example: Scissor sweep from closed guard, x-pass to knee on belly, Lapel choke from side control, butterfly guard sweep, etc. It is also important that you make the name/title of the technique stand out. You can do this by writing the name in all capital, bold, highlighted, or underlined lettering. The important aspect here is that it stands out to you. This way, when you look back to your notes, it will be easy to locate a specific move for review.

If your coach is teaching you a set of move options from a specific set up, note the set up first, then list the varying options.

It is important to detail each specific grip type in your narration as follows:

Grips:
- Thumb in grip
- Four fingers in grip
- C-grip
- Pistol grip
- Gable grip

- Monkey grip

Hooks:
- Spider hook
- De La Riva hook
- Underhook
- Overhook
- **Butterfly hook**

Note: *Not all grip and hook types are listed.*

In notebook, always distinguish your left from your right side, for yourself and drilling partner. An example of this would be:

I have my opponent in my closed guard. My right hand gets a pistol grip of o's left sleeve.

Using shortened, abbreviated terms ("o" for opponent) will help to minimalize note taking time.

It is not necessary to purchase a journal/notebook specific to BJJ. Any composition, or spiral bound notebook will suffice.

Honest Self-Inventory

Taking a self-inventory is doing a self-evaluation of specific areas that you are good at, and also recognizing specific holes in your game that need attention/focus. It is important that you are honest in your evaluation. The main objective in your evaluation should be in identifying obstacles that are hindering your progress. You should also take the time necessary to write down these issues, so you can formulate a drilling and training game plan to combat the problem.

It is also an excellent idea to ask your instructor what he/she sees in regard to specific areas that may need improvement/focus. Their expertise can typically point out areas of needed improvement that you may overlook.

Also, listen to the upper belts in your class. They usually will offer insight and ideas that will help your progression.

Some specifics to look for:

- What obstacles are you running into when attempting specific guard types, and guard passes?

- What submissions do you get caught in most?

- Where are you feeling most frustration?

- What positions are hardest for you to escape?

Do Your Homework

I could not be adamant enough about the importance of doing your homework as a jiu-jitsu practitioner. It will be very hard to progress through arising plateaus in your game if you do not take the time to do your homework.

There are many online resources, books, magazines and DVDs that will help you take your jiu-jitsu game to the next level. Look for the learning material that will effectively supplement your game. Not all are created equal. There are usually reviews and discussion boards online that will help you make the proper selection.

Although it is important to learn multiple guards and passing styles, make sure you dedicate time to sharpening your fundamentals. This is the foundation that you need to build on. If a house is built on a weak foundation, it cannot stand. There is always details that will improve what you are already good at in regard to BJJ fundamentals. If you can truly perfect your execution of a specific technique to a great degree, you will be more confident in its use and application in live sparring, competition, and self-defense.

Also, if you have the availability to drill technique at home, this will be a great advantage in your development. Family members, or friends may let you work some drills. If you are lacking willing participants, investing in a jiu-jitsu dummy could be a great way to drill technique at home.

Note: *I recommend getting an economical training mat for drilling technique at home.*

Detail

What makes, or breaks the effectiveness of any move in jiu-jitsu is attention to detail. There are a lot of intricate details that can easily go overlooked, if you are not paying attention. I have noticed and learned early, that it is only a matter of a small detail in factors, that will determine the success, or failure of any specific move. Paying attention to the minor details will help you become better in your training and competitive fights. Some specific details to look for are:

- Positional

- Grip type (pistol, thumb in, four finger in, gable, etc.)
- Posture

- Timing

- Pressure placement (hips, shoulder, knee, head, hands, etc.)

Take the time to drill technique correctly. Missing even one aspect of detail will prevent your success in implementation. Sometimes a move can be improperly judged by an individual practitioner as being ineffective, but in reality, the technique is successful when correctly executed.

Be On the Attack

The more you implement your game, the less opportunity your opponent has to work his/her game plan on you. I like to keep my opponents on the constant defense. This limits their opportunity to progress in position and submission.

Limit Dwell Time:

Avoid stalling when rolling, or competing. When you stall during a roll, or a match, you offer your training partners and opponents the necessary time to create space, escape, counter, or reverse the position.

Attack the Defense:

Being on the attack also creates additional exposures for attack when your opponent attempts to defend. For example, their protecting the neck may create availability for you to attack the arm. In contrast, protecting the arm may create opportunity to attack the neck.

Control the Fight:

Being on the attack also allows you the opportunity to dictate where you want the roll (sparring) to go. If you want to train a specific area of your jiu-jitsu, taking the roll where you want it presents the option of choosing what part of your game you want to work on.

Plan of Attack:

Have a plan before coming into class of what you specifically want to accomplish in your training for that day. This pertains to the sparring (rolling) portion of the class. Have a plan of attack for what guard types, positional control, passes, submissions, etc. that you want to work on.

Grip Fighting

Grip Fighting (establishing/breaking grips):

My very first objective when I roll with training partners, or compete, is to establish my grips specific to the technique I will use. Whether you are starting from your feet, or from the ground, your success in sweeps, passes, takedowns, arm drags, guard pulls, etc., will be dependent upon you first establishing proper grips.

At the same time, it is important that you do not allow your opponents, or training partners to establish their grips. If someone gets their grips in on you, or a single grip, always immediately break the grip(s), and counter

grip. By getting your grips in first, you will be in a position to be on the attack to implement your game. This is always better than having someone work their game plan out on you.

Break Grips (attacking/defensive grips):

Spend dedicated time learning techniques for breaking grips and countering grips. This is not only in relation to playing guard, and passing guard, but in breaking your opponent's attacking grips (e.g. lapel chokes) and grip defense.

A typical grip defense that is seen on the mats, is when attacking for the armbar. Your opponent may use a lapel grip, gable grip, or other varying defensive grip types to prevent your submission attempt. Instead of using energy depleting strength that is mostly ineffective at combatting grip defense, there is a number of simple, but effective grip breaking techniques that will help to circumvent the obstacle in achieving the submission.

Pressure/Weight Distribution

The key to a successful top game and many of BJJ's guard passes, are directly connected to the proper application of pressure. Knowing how and where to distribute your weight will bring your jiu-jitsu game to a whole new level.

I have rolled with a variety of training partners of varying size, strength, ranks and levels. One thing that I noticed early in my training is the incredible amount of pressure that even the smallest/lightest training partners could generate. This is more typical with higher ranking jiu-jitsu practitioners (purple, brown, and black belts). I would be rolling with someone that was anywhere from approximately 130 to 150 lbs., and to me it would feel like 300 lbs. of bricks were sitting on me. This pressure made it extremely difficult to implement my route for escape.

I would talk to my training partners after a roll, and they would tell me that their game plan is to create such an immense amount of pressure on their opponents, that they would almost willingly give up position, or submission to relieve the pressure that was created by their proper weight distribution.

Constantly be aware of how pressure plays a role in your jiu-jitsu game. When you are always looking for how/where you rest your hips, shoulder, knee, and even head in relation to creating pressure, your techniques will be solid.

Muscle Memory

As I have shared before, drilling technique will allow you to develop muscle memory. This is so important to your jiu-jitsu success. You do not want to be in a position where you have to actively concentrate on each individual step to effectively utilize a specific move.

Drilling without resistance is the first necessary step in committing a technique to muscle memory. The only way to truly solidify the techniques you have been drilling to muscle memory, is to add it to your rolling (live sparring) game. This is a necessary step that typically goes overlooked. You may have drilled a technique a 100 plus times, but have yet to put it into action in your rolling. If muscle memory is the ability to reproduce a technique without conscious thought, then it can only become reactionary as it is practiced with full resistance (rolling). It is in the implementation and practice of the technique in constant usage, that you will see the move become reactionary.

Ultimately, muscle memory allows you to execute technique naturally, by reflex, and with more confidence. You will see yourself accomplishing your game plan and better adapt to the unforeseen that your opponents will present to you when you have committed your technique to muscle memory.

Mental Drilling

Mental drilling is a concept that enables you to take the technique you trained in class and play the steps carefully in your mind. As you ponder/meditate on each step of a technique, you greatly increase your retention level.

- Find the right time for mental drilling. It is important to do this during your personal down time. The best time to implement this exercise, is when you are laying down in bed, right before sleep.
- Make sure that your environment is conducive to this exercise. Eliminate any possible distractions.
- Recall a specific move that you just learned, or are learning. This could be from a recent class.
- Play each step of the move in proper sequence. Be mindful to include each step. Missing any detail will prevent you from properly learning the technique.
- Give yourself plenty of reps. In allowing your mind to replay a move, over and over, you will commit the sequence to memory.

Mental drilling is concentrating on each isolated step of technique in your mind. This allows you to mentally visualize the process of execution. The more time you spend recalling a recent technique in mental drilling, the deeper the move will be impressed upon your mind for physical drilling and rolling.

Having a Well-Rounded Game

Guard Game:

What I have noticed in the duration of my training, is that jiu-jitsu practitioners that are really good, have a well-rounded game. This means that they are familiar with and effectively use multiple guard types. This is especially true with black belts.

It is important to know the benefits of each guard type. This is only accomplished by practice and use of its application. By understanding how to effectively work a specific guard type through application, you will know its benefits, strengths, and potential vulnerabilities.

Passing guard:

It can be difficult to know how to effectively pass a guard that you haven't spent time with on the opposite side, playing guard. I know how to pass the closed guard with success, because I have spent a lot of time with training partners in my closed guard. I have recognized and know what my opponent is looking for (grips, posture, etc.) to initiate their pass for the closed guard.

Game Development:

Avoid the pitfalls of being one-dimensional in your game development. Sometimes jiu-jitsu practitioners can get too comfortable putting all their time into one area of their training. It is that comfort level that will hinder your progress. Add new guard types that you are unfamiliar with that will supplement your overall development. This will add a new dimension to your game. If you are most comfortable playing from your back, spend extra time developing your passing game (from standing). The only way to become a well-rounded jiu-jitsu fighter, is to stretch your development beyond your comfort level.

The Advanced Game

For beginners in jiu-jitsu, the focus in learning is mostly on fundamental singular moves, and establishing correct positions. Advanced game fighters have surpassed the fundamental basics in the development of their game.

The following qualities constitutes an advanced game fighter:

- Fundamental knowledge and execution of technique (fundamentals are foundational to the advanced fighter game).
- Having a variety of options for each guard type and passing style.
- The adaptability to circumvent defensive barriers and obstacles.
- Having a variety of escape options from each positional control type and submission attempt; an altogether tight defense and guard retention game.
- The proper application and use of pressure.

Additionally, the advanced game includes: having multiple routes, connecting the dots (putting an effective game plan together), and sneaky jiu-jitsu (creating exposures for attack).

Having Multiple Routes

Having multiple routes is the ability to effectively work a guard, pass, submission, etc., regardless of what is presented you in a match, or rolling. To do this, it is important to know a variety of options from different scenarios you will face in your training. When you are an advanced fighter, you should have a list of options at your disposal for any type of guard you play, or guard you intend to pass. If you feel any of your options are limited, then it is time to focus on implementing some new techniques. For instance, if your closed guard retention is only effective until your opponent tries to initiate a standing guard pass, you have work to do. An advanced player should be able to adapt to whatever is presented and have an answer for each situation.

Connecting the Dots

Being able to connect the dots is bringing all the pieces together. It is changing from the rigid singular moves to manifesting true "arte suave" (the gentle art). This is being able to smoothly transition between all aspects of your jiu-jitsu game. The ability to flow from one position to the next, or from sweep, right into submission should be natural. There are certain aspects of training that will help in this.

Chain Drilling:

This is a training technique that combines a list of moves connected in a longer sequence. A good way to start is transitioning between all the fundamental positions (side control, north-south, knee on belly, mount, etc.). You should then start to implement more complex sequences.

Flow Rolling:

The objective with flow rolling is not really about fighting for submission as you see in live sparring (rolling). It is more a way for you to smoothly transition between all aspects of jiu-jitsu with your training partner with limited resistance. This training exercise is a way that you and your training partner can transition back and forth in sweeps, passes, escapes, counters, submissions. Your jiu-jitsu should look smooth to those spectating.

Ultimate Result:

When you have connected the dots in your development, you will see how every aspect of your training creates the full picture in BJJ. Every practitioner's picture may differ depending on how they adapt their specific body style to the game they put together. This is the beautiful thing about jiu-jitsu; no fighter's game (picture) is exactly the same.

Sneaky Jiu-Jitsu

Sneaky jiu-jitsu is a concept of creating exposures that your opponents are not expecting. You could make it appear that you are attempting a certain submission, when in reality you are fishing for a certain reaction from your opponent that will facilitate an exposure you need to achieve your intended submission. One example of sneaky jiu-jitsu that I like to use is in the following:

Sneaky Triangle from Closed Guard:

My opponent is in my closed guard. My right hand gets a cross grip of my opponent's right sleeve. I reach down with my left hand and get a grip of the side of my opponent's gi pants just below their right knee. I use my left hand grip to pull myself to a 90-degree angle with the back of my left leg moving against the right lat of my opponent. At this point, they are thinking *omo plata*. Maintaining my grips, I pressure my left leg against the side of my opponent's right lat. The unconscious reaction of my opponent is to base out his/her left arm to counter the pressure I am putting into him/her, so they won't fall to the left. This is exactly the reaction I was looking for. This exposure that I intended to create, opened up perfect access for me to apply the triangle. My right leg now has an opening to come through and come across my opponent's neck, being in perfect position to finish my submission. I won't cover the fundamentals of completing the triangle choke submission.

The Guard

There is a great number of guard types in BJJ. They consist of, but are not limited to the following:

- Closed guard
- Half guard
- Butterfly guard
- De La Riva guard
- Reverse De La Riva
- Spider guard
- Lasso guard
- Cross guard
- Open guard
- Inverted guard
- Deep Half
- 50/50 guard
- X guard
- Worm guard
- Lapel guard

Your primary goal in establishing your guard is to get your grips and hooks in. Your grips/hooks will vary depending on the type of guard you intend to employ. For example, spider guard is established with sleeve grips, while counter pressuring your feet (blade of foot) against the inside of your training partner's elbows. Butterfly guard may call for you to get an underhook with your right arm, while getting a sleeve grip with your left hand. With this guard, you will also be using what can be referred to as a butterfly hook (front of ankle/foot hooking inside of your training partner's leg).

Now that your guard has been established, there are two objectives you need to accomplish to have an effective guard, and these are key. They are; breaking posture, and off balancing of your opponent (taking away your opponent's base).

Breaking Posture:

When your opponent has posture, he/she is strong. When your opponent's posture is broken down, they are vulnerable to control, sweeps, and submissions.

There are a variety of posture breaking techniques that can be used. Some of these are:

- Head control
- Underhooks
- Pulling down on lapel.
- Pulling sleeve.
- Arm drag
- Counter pressure (stretching your opponent out)
- Pulling inside of elbows.
- Transition to a high guard (from closed guard).

It will be difficult for your opponent to defend the submission if his/her posture is properly broken down. Secondly, your opponent cannot even begin to initiate a guard pass until they reestablish and maintain posture.

If you have attempted a submission from the guard and failed, it is usually because you haven't properly broken your opponent's posture down before attempting the submission.

Depending upon what guard you are using, when your opponent has strong, stubborn posture, there is usually a transitionary moment that you should look for that will allow you to be effective with breaking your opponent down. For example, my opponent is in my closed guard. Their posture is correct and grips are established in preparation to pass the guard. The transitionary moment that I am looking for, is when my opponent goes to L their legs (putting knee behind tailbone and angle out opposite knee at a ninety-degree angle to break guard for the pass). Usually your opponent will come up and slightly lean forward in this brief moment, so they can shift their knees into L position. This allows you to capitalize on a small moment where their posture is compromised, to easily break their posture. Accomplish this before they can actually get their knees into the L position.

There are other options to deal with stubborn posture. Sometimes it is easier to work with what is dealt to you. An effective sweep from the closed guard when you are dealing with good posture is to initiate a hip bump sweep to mount. If your opponent tries to defend this and pressures back into you, then you can pull them back down into your closed guard with broken posture.

Off-Balancing Your Opponent:

Taking away your opponent's base is what allows you to sweep your opponent. When your opponent has a solid base, he/she is not going anywhere.

Some ways to off-balance your opponent are:

- Misdirection
- Getting under your opponent.
- Stretch opponent out (counter pressure).
- Controlling limbs with sleeve grip, pant grip, wrist control, etc. This limits the options for your opponent to base out, or post, in defending the sweep.

Passing the Guard

There are a variety of guards that you will have to deal with. Some are more common than others.

Posture and Base:

Your very first objective in passing the guard is maintaining correct base and posture. This pertains to either making your entry for the pass, or if you are already inside your opponent's guard.

Removing Hooks/Grips:

Your next objective is to remove any hooks and grips that your opponent has established. If your opponent has grips and hooks in, he/she may be able to start affecting your posture and base. Unless you strip the grips and clear the hooks, it will only be a matter of time before your opponent will start attacking for sweeps, or submissions.

Establish Grips/Re-grip:

Upon any guard pass entry, immediately establish your grips. While in the guard, if you have successfully removed/stripped your opponent's grips, immediately re-grip.

If at this time your opponent again, affects your posture, gets hooks in, or reestablishes grips, then start the beginning fundamental steps for passing guard.

Adapt to Reaction:

Now that you have shut down your opponent's guard to an extent, this does not mean you are out of danger. As you begin your pass, you may need to adapt to their reaction. Their reaction may call for you to switch to the opposite side to complete your guard pass. You may need to employ a completely different guard pass.

A good training partner could transition between multiple guard types while you are attempting to pass their guard. This could become very frustrating if you don't have the adaptability to work with what is blocking your progress while passing. Your guard passing game should be just as dynamic as your guard game if you want to progress in jiu-jitsu.

Openings for Guard Types and Attacks

Look for and recognize openings for guard types. When someone is new to jiu-jitsu, it can be difficult to know what guard will be effective in certain situations. When beginning a roll, look for what starting position your training partner is in. This should help you know what options you have to effectively respond.

Both Knees:

- Closed guard
- Butterfly guard
- Low takedowns
- Knee shield
- Open guard variations

Note: *I don't recommend ever approaching a roll starting from both knees. This is not a good attacking position, and leaves you vulnerable to getting taken off balance.*

Combat Base:

- Spider/Shin to Shin combo
- De La Riva guard (thread DLR hook through forward leg)
- Low takedown (ankle pull-shoulder push)
- Open guard variations

Note: *If your partner starts in combat base with their right leg forward, and you are in a seated variation, grab your partner's forward right ankle with your left hand and thread your left leg through to set up De La Riva guard.*

Seated:

- Berimbolo
- 50/50
- Knee shield
- Low takedowns
- Open guard variations

Standing:

When your training partner is standing and you are in a seated position, any number of open guard types may be employed. If both you, and your training partner start from standing, your options are to work a takedown, pull guard, and for advanced practitioners, flying attacks (flying armbar, flying triangle, etc.).

Guard Retention

Guard retention is such an important part of your success in BJJ. A lot of times we limit our view and understanding of the guard to just the basic idea of establish guard, sweep, and submit. Your guard should be dynamic and reactionary to the potential dangers that are presented to you from your opponents. Your guard should be to first control your opponent, and limit/reduce any progress your opponent is intending. If your opponent starts to attempt a guard pass, shutting down their progress with your guard, in retaining guard, is going to be a lot easier than trying to escape a solid side control, mount, etc. The following may assist you in your guard retention success:

Going Inverted:

Although this may require some level of flexibility, going inverted could be very frustrating for anyone's attempts on passing the guard.

Transitioning to an Alternate Guard:

Some guards that work well in transition are closed guard to any variation of open guard (Spider guard, Lasso guard, Lapel guard, etc.) Transitioning between De La Riva and Reverse De La Riva guards are also effective in guard retention. With transitioning between guard types, using your feet and grips to create barriers in stopping guard pass progress is key.

Granby Roll:

If you are not familiar with this technique, you should definitely add it to your guard retention game. This is fundamental to thwarting guard passes.

Barriers & Walls:

The most effective way to shut down your opponent's guard passing progress, is by creating barriers (walls) with your feet, knees, hands, forearms, etc., to control the distance. Some points of contact for creating barriers are:

- Feet on the hips, shoulders and biceps.
- Hand hooking the back of neck with forearm across side of neck/trap (this creates a blocking check in seated guard, or combat base variations).
- Knees against shoulders, or hips when blocking low guard passes.
- Hands with straight arm against traps when opponent is low on your hips, or head at stomach (usually seen when an opponent attempts to pass butterfly guard, or when they try to pass low with an over-under pass).
- Hand(s) hooking with forearm(s) blocking opponent's crossface attempts.

- Hand straight arming opponent's hip (be mindful to use this barrier only when your arm is not susceptible to armlock).

The Mount

It has been said before that when you have the mount, to flow like water. This may not be anything new, or groundbreaking, but is an accurate saying. Allow your mount pressure to move with your opponent. You may need to transition from a high mount to a technical mount to achieve your end goal. Understanding the mount types will assist in this regard.

Grape Vine – For Low Mount:

This is essentially hooking the back of your opponent's legs when you have the low mount. The more you contract your grapevine hooks, the more mount pressure you place on your opponent's hips.

Technical Mount:

This is a great transitionary mount to attack from. The opportunity to transition into a technical mount typically comes from escape attempts where your opponent is on his/her side. This position also gives you excellent access to take the back.

High Mount:

When you get the high mount, make sure to get your knees high under your opponent's arms to limit their ability to create a frame. Avoid sitting below the sternum, as this presents the space needed for your opponent to effectively bridge and employ escapes.

Stay Busy:

The more time your opponent's focus is on defending continual attacks on the neck, the shoulder (americana), or the arm, the less opportunity they will have to work an escape. The key here is to stay busy.

The only mount position where it would be acceptable to take your time is the low mount. This is due to the immense top pressure that grapevine hooks can create.

The Back Mount

There is a reason why the back mount is of the highest scoring positions in sport jiu-jitsu. It is arguably the most dominant position in BJJ.

Once back mount is achieved, the objective is to maintain control. The following is helpful in this regard:

Seat Belt:

The seat belt grip is fundamental in taking back control. Make sure that when you have the seat belt established, to keep tight head positioning to your opponent. Also, eliminate any space that can be used for escape by keeping your body aligned with your opponent.

The Kimura grip:

This grip offers excellent wrist control from the back. The kimura grip additionally enables you to attack for an armbar from the back. This is especially effective, because defensive focus is typically concentrated on protecting the neck.

Active Hooks:

Use your hooks to stretch your opponent out in conjunction with hip pressure. Your hooks are not meant to remain in an inactive, rigid state. With back control, you may need to hook behind the knee of your opponent for additional control. The type of lower body methods of control should be dynamic and reactionary.

The Body Triangle:

Establishing a body triangle is an excellent option for controlling the back. A tightly secured body triangle has the potential to generate a great amount of pressure, and can lead to submission. Although submitting your opponent from a body triangle is uncommon, the pressure that is created may draw attention away from defending their neck.

Also, with the body triangle, hooking the opponent's leg behind the knee with your free leg offers additional control.

A Successful Side Control

Head Down:

Always keep your head down. This eliminates the space your opponent needs to create pressure against your neck with their forearm. Typically, this is their primary objective for escaping side control.

Hip Pressure:

Hip pressure is paramount in achieving a solid side control. Your hip pressure should be resting on your opponent's hips, as to balance all your body's weight on a single point.

Your hip pressure can also be used on your opponent's shoulders when transitioning to a reverse scarf hold position.

Pinning the Shoulders:

Your opponent cannot initiate an escape without getting to their side. This is impossible to do when their shoulders are pinned to the mat. Use shoulder pressure, underhooks, and the cross face to keep control of your opponent's shoulders.

Also, using your opponent's lapel may offer additional control in pinning the shoulders. Having side control when training in the gi, pull your opponents lapel out with the hand/arm you have underhooking, and pass the lapel to your cross face palm down hand under your opponent's shoulder. Be sure that there is no slack in the lapel. Using this type of control is an excellent way to keep your opponent's shoulders pinned to the mat.

Balls of Feet:

Create additional top pressure by getting on the balls of your feet when controlling your opponent in side control. It is important to drive forward from your feet to generate the pressure, and target the pressure on a specific point (hips, chest, shoulders, etc.).

Competition Prep

Game plan:

When putting together a game plan, it is important to stick with what has been proven to be effective for you on the mats during training. Create a game plan that includes set ups, passes, guard sweeps, and submissions that you have a high success rate with. It is not time to implement new, or flashy techniques that you are not familiar with.

If you have any weak, or vulnerable areas in your game, it is time to shore it up. For example, if you are constantly getting pinned down in half guard, you need to work on some effective guard retention and escapes from the half guard position. There is always a good chance you will be facing competitors that can capitalize on your weak areas.

Dieting/Cutting Weight:

Do not be tempted to get too outrageous with your dieting program. I recommend that you register at a weight class that your body is already close to. You do not want to step on the competition mat feeling depleted due to improper dieting practices. Your energy and strength levels need to be at their peak, so that you can perform at your best. Cutting weight too quickly will rob you of this. Eating a clean diet will keep your body competition ready and increase your overall health.

Some basic dieting fundamentals for eating clean:

Avoid:

- Sugar (candy, cake, soda, etc.)
- high glycemic carbs (white bread, white rice, bagels, potatoes, etc.)
- Processed foods
- Fast food
- Fatty meats (bacon, sausage, ground beef, etc.)

Include:

- Complex carbohydrates (oats, brown rice, quinoa, amaranth, sweet potatoes,100% whole grains)
- Lean meats (fish, chicken breast, etc.)
- Fruits and vegetables

Note: *If you choose to fry foods, this should be done in only a coconut, or canola oil. Recent studies prove that extra virgin olive oil can only maintain its positive nutritional properties in its raw form.*

Starting from Your Feet

We are ground fighters, but we should at least be comfortable starting on our feet. One of the anxieties that some jiu-jitsu fighters face prior to a jiu-jitsu match is the foreboding wonder if your opponent is also a high level judoka. I don't worry about many judo fighters once I am already on the ground, but getting thrown to the mat would not be a great way to start a competition fight. Unfortunately, some BJJ academies altogether stay away from starting from your feet. I understand that mat space is an important factor that will determine whether a jiu-jitsu professor decides on how his students will initiate live sparring (rolling). There is also less opportunity for student injury for academies that start from their knees. I do appreciate when an academy spends time, or days specific to throws/takedowns and the associated counters to such.

The following will create more confidence when starting from a standing position during a roll, or competition:

Drilling breakfalls:

There is nothing more paramount to your success and confidence on your feet as a jiu-jitsu fighter than committing fundamental breakfall technique to your muscle memory. The knowledge and practice of breakfalls takes away the potential sting of getting thrown by dissipating the impact and energy of the throw through the extension of proper body reaction and position. It is the difference of a smooth dive into water, as opposed to a hard belly flop.

Train Judo:

Although Brazilian Jiu-Jitsu incorporates a lot of the throws and technique you will find in a judo dojo, BJJ is specialized to ground fighting. If your BJJ academy does not dedicate time/training to throws, takedowns, and counters to such, it may be a good idea to add some additional training at your local judo club. However, I would recommend you first seek the help of your BJJ instructor, because they usually have a sound knowledge of the afore mentioned techniques.

Transition Submission
Countering Submission Defense

There is a clear path between armbar, triangle, and omo plata in the closed guard, depending on how your opponent reacts to your submission attempts. From side control, you should be able to flow from americana, straight arm lock, and kimura. From mount, you can transition from x choke to armbar, or americana to armbar, and so on.

One of my favorite transition submissions is from the mount. I transition from armbar to bow & arrow choke.

It is important to understand and recognize how submissions work together. In higher level jiu-jitsu, it is not common to tap out your training partners/opponents off of your first submission attempt. With this in mind, your first attempt at submission is really used for set up purposes. Attempting an americana from mount creates a vulnerability for your opponent's opposite arm when they try to reach over and defend the submission. Reaching their arm over to defend the americana exposes your opponent's reaching arm to an armbar.

Again, understand that your first submission attempt is probably not going to tap your opponents out. It is important that you learn how to counter and capitalize on submission defense that is presented to you.

Using Submission as a Controlling Position

There are a few submissions that can also act as a controlling position. The omo plata and triangle are the most common. The triangle from guard is especially effective as a controlling position.

If my opponent gives me a hard time in my attempt to finish the triangle, I use my triangle as a controlling position. In this position, my opponent is thinking *defend the triangle* when I have other options in mind.

For the triangle position to work, make sure that you are angled out at ninety degrees to your opponent. You should be looking directly into your opponent's ear. From this position, it is easy to attack the free arm for the following submissions:

- Kimura lock

- Straight arm lock (isolate your opponent's forearm against the side of your neck and pressure with hooking arm against the back of opponent's elbow)

- Wrist lock variations

There are also a lot of attacks you can employ on your opponent's arm that is trapped inside the triangle. These consist of the following submissions:

- Armbar from triangle position

- Key lock (getting a two handed grip on the wrist, isolate your opponent's elbow against your abdominal wall when their arm is contracted in an angle; torque your opponent's wrist in the proper direction to achieve submission)

- Wrist lock variations

Reactionary Cues

Although BJJ is often compared to the game of chess, jiu-jitsu does not offer you an excess amount of time to formulate your next move. This is why it is so important that your jiu-jitsu game is reactionary. You have to train your mind to quickly recognize and respond to your opponent by reflex.

In live sparring and competition, recognizing specific key moments should elicit an automatic response. These mental triggers are reactionary cues for you to immediately employ specific technique options for response. The timing that is needed to effectuate an automatic response is developed during the rolling portion of your class.

There are certain reactions you need to recognize from your opponent that tell you it is time to sweep, to counter, or to submit. Look at the following two example of reactionary ques.

Example one:

Your opponent is in your closed guard. They posture straight up, or may even lean a back a little bit. This is a reactionary cue that tells you to initiate a hip bump sweep.

Example two:

Another easy example is when your opponent is in your closed guard and places one of their hands on the mat. This reactionary cue should elicit an automatic response to attack for the kimura.

As reactionary cues are committed to muscle memory, these situational mental triggers will present great opportunity for automatic offensive and defensive tactics.

Pulling Sweep

Pulling a sweep allows you to bypass the step of establishing guard, to then have to work for a sweep. This concept is a good way to take your training partner, or opponent off guard. An example of an effective sweep pull, is pulling the scissor sweep. This works well when rolling, and your training partner starts from their knees. Once you have quickly established your grips associated with the scissor sweep, it is just a matter of shooting your legs into position, and following through for the sweep.

Pulling sweep should not be a regular part of your everyday game. What makes pulling a sweep effective is that it is unexpected, having an element of surprise.

Be mindful that pulling sweep has the potential to generate an increased amount of force/impact to your training partner's back against the mat, that is typically associated with a standing takedown.

Plateaus/Walls

As you progress in your BJJ training, you may start to notice your strengths and weaknesses. It is normal for one to play on their strengths in any competitive situation. Although, avoiding weak areas in technique and game plan will create a wall/plateau in your training.

I am sure that your regular training partners will start to notice your strengths and weaknesses as well. This makes you vulnerable, because it will be their goal to capitalize on your weaknesses.

If you're having trouble recognizing your weak areas, look for the following:

- Comfort level in position
  If you are feeling particularly vulnerable in a position, this can be a clear indicator of a weak area.

- Frequency of submission
  What specific submissions do you get caught in, and how often?

- Limited Options
  If you only have one, or two options for escape, sweep, guard pass, submission, etc. from any

particular area of jiu-jitsu, there is a definite need for improvement.

- Where you get stuck
  If you are unable to effectuate a pass to any of the varying guard types, or when you're spending too much time in someone's positional control, this is an indication of a plateau.

Now that you have recognized the plateaus/walls in your development, it is time to put together a concentrated game plan to overcome this barrier.

Focused drilling:

Learn the technique specific to your weak area and refine(sharpen) the techniques you already have a knowledge of. Seek the help of your BJJ instructor, and implement the information found in the "Do Your Homework" section of this book. Drill the technique(s) without missing any detail. Give yourself a set time in days/weeks for drilling to commit the technique(s) to muscle memory.

When Rolling:

It is important that you allow yourself to be put in challenging situations that will facilitate growth. When difficulties are avoided, then you are just delaying potential for development.

Set your starting point from an area that you are focused at getting better. For example, if your bottom half-guard needs improvement, set the starting point of your roll from bottom half-guard. When a guard pass is the focus, start inside your training partner's guard.

The Ultimate Result:

You will know that you have made it over the plateau, or through a wall in your development when you handle prior weak areas with comfort and confidence. This is due to the new and refined options that negate your opponent's progress.

Muscle Strength

Muscle strength can play a positive role in jiu-jitsu. It is nowhere on the level of importance to that of technique. To be clear, muscle strength should not be anything a jiu-jitsu practitioner should ever rely on. It is technique that is of utmost importance in your BJJ success. Utilizing correct technique is what can give you the advantage over your opponents, and is what can level the playing field between strong and weak fighters.

Strength Training

I do not recommend gimmicky, or trendy workout routines. I won't say that you won't get any results from swinging a kettle ball around, or balancing on a ball, but your results will be minimal at best. In all reality, they haven't done much in the way of increasing strength and body composition. Conventional weight training is paramount to developing strength and an aesthetic body.

Developing Grip Strength:

- Hammer curls
- Wrist curls
- Reverse wrist curls
- Belt pull ups

- Rope pull ups

Note: *It is important to use weight that allows you to get a full contraction within the full range of motion of the exercise. Keep movements slow and controlled to avoid cheating (swinging weights)*

Developing Core Strength:

Your core strength, which mainly consist of your abdominal wall, abdominal obliques, and lower back play an important role in BJJ.
All of your fundamental moves (bridging, hip escapes, etc.), guard passes, playing guard, and more, rely on core strength.

Some recommended core strength training:

Abdominal wall:
- Crunches
- Hanging leg raises
- Planks (isometric training is also an important part of core development)
- Cable crunches
- triangles

Abdominal obliques:
- Dumbbell side bends
- Oblique cable crunches

- Side plank
- Plate twist (on decline bench)

Lower back:
- Deadlift
- Hip extensions
- Squat (this compound exercise, although mainly focuses on quads and glutes, does promote lower back strength and stability)

Although the strength portion of this book focuses on a few key areas of training specific for jiu-jitsu, it is recommended to incorporate a weight training schedule to include your full body throughout the week. Having a strong body is essential to injury prevention and overall health.

Cardio & Jiu-Jitsu

For anyone that is already familiar with BJJ training, you know the cardio level (fitness level) that is required. Your cardio level is the size of your gas tank. Some methods to increase cardio are listed in the following:

- Class attendance (the more you train, the more you condition your body to adapt to the rigors of training)
- Proper diet

- Cardio vascular training (running, jogging, biking, HIIT, swimming, etc.)
- Adequate rest
- Abstaining from alcoholic beverages and smoking.

Fatigue

There are a number of reasons anyone will feel the effects of fatigue. They are; improper diet, lack of sleep, overtraining, dehydration, and lack of overall fitness level.

Because jiu-jitsu is a fighting style that utilizes the mind, fatigue does not only effect the muscle endurance, it effects the mind.

Fatigue slows down your reaction time, and wears down your will to keep going.

Energy Conservation

There are a few items that will help in your energy conservation.

Most energy sapping moments in BJJ happen when under the pressure of a solid mount, side control, knee on belly, back mount, or north-south position.

The most effective way to avoid energy draining moments to begin with, is to prevent them from ever happening. To prevent getting in energy sapping positions from your opponent, you need an effective guard, and effective guard retention.

Wait for the right moment to implement a bridge, or hip bump. There are transitionary moments that your opponents will give you that will be optimal for escapes in energy retention. These are very short moments, and you only have a small window of opportunity to capitalize on what is presented to you.

Going Light

In addition to the obvious methods (sleep, hydration, exercise, and proper diet), an effective way to combat fatigue is to go light.

It is not recommended that you go hard every training session. You must give your body opportunity to recover. Being depleted due to overtraining will affect your mental retention level when drilling. It will also affect your performance when rolling, or competing.

It is good to train at a higher intensity level at times. This is especially true for competition prep. As shared before, it is not recommended to train at extreme levels all the time. Your body needs time to recover.

If you train regularly, and are feeling the effects of fatigue, go light. The important thing to do is pay close attention to your body. Brazilian Jiu-Jitsu can take a toll on your energy levels.

You may even need to take a day off to fully recover.

Ex 20:11 For in six days the Lord made heaven and earth, the sea, and all that in them is, and rested the seventh day.

It is important to take a day off from training. This way you will come back to the mats fresh.

Injuries

A hard reality for any jiu-jitsu practitioner is that there is the risk of injury. Most injuries you may see on the mat are quite minor. However, it is possible to get a more debilitating injury during training, or competition. Hopefully this section will convey some information that may decrease, or eliminate the occurrence of potential injury.

Injury prevention:

The best way to deal with injury is to prevent it from ever happening. To do this, you must train smart. Some key points that will assist you in training safely are listed in the following:

Tap Often/Tap Early:

Pride is usually the number one culprit for injury on the mats. Pride is what leads jiu-jitsu practitioners to hold out when it is time to tap. Trying to hold out on a submission that you have no route for escape will quickly lead to an injury. You do not have to wait until the submissions, such as; armbar, kimura, americana, kneebar, ankle lock, or omo plata are fully extended before tapping. Sometimes it is best to tap early if you know you got caught with a quick submission. You should do this well before your training partner has opportunity to really crank down. There are escapes for all these, but I do not recommend hanging out in a submission attempt if you don't have a good grasp of the specifics/fundamentals required for the escape technique needed.

Also, if you have a choke set in, or no route for a quick escape, you should tap early as well. You don't want to wait until you start to black out, or see stars, before you tap to a choke. It will usually be too late at that point.

Another good habit in training safely is to not only tap with your hand, but to verbally say tap. This way, if your hands are tied up, your training partners will know to release the submission.

Don't Be a Spaz:

The times that I have mostly seen a jiu-jitsu practitioners injure themselves, or others, is when they spaz out. Those who spaz out overly exert themselves with explosive moves and strength to compensate for their lack of technique. In this spastic state, it is difficult for one to maintain the body awareness needed to train safely.

Thankfully, these types are not too commonly seen on the training mats. Spazzes are usually a rare white belt that still needs to overcome pride. Unfortunately, I have seen an occasional blue belt display this behavior. Spazzes are easy to spot out, and mostly avoided in class. Your training partners will typically train safely.

Remember that BJJ is the gentle art (arte suave). Trying to plow through your training partners with brute strength will not allow you to learn proper technique, and can only lead to injury for yourself and others.

Proper Protective Gear

Protective gear is another option that can be used to limit injury. The most typical used at jiu-jitsu academies are:

Mouth Guard:

I recommend using a mouth guard when rolling. It should be a requirement at BJJ competitions.

Ear Protection:

Some BJJ practitioners are more prone to cauliflower ear than others. If you want to avoid the potential for cauliflower ear, wear ear guards. Some fighters accept banged up ears as a badge of honor. I recommend checking with your significant other to see what they would like.

Finger Taping:

Regular jiu-jitsu training can put a lot of stress on your joints. This is especially true with practitioners that train with the gi. Using jiu-jitsu tape (athletic tape) may alleviate some of the potential wear and tear on your finger joints associated with regular training.

I also find that utilizing a pistol grip, as opposed to four finger in grip, when applicable, greatly reduces any stress that may impact your finger joints when rolling, or competing.

Training While Injured

It shows great focus and dedication to actively attend class when injured. Some important guidelines to follow when injured are:

Communicate your injury and physical limitations with your instructor and training partners before drilling, or rolling.

Know your limits. You may have to sit on the side lines and observe technique while recovering from an injury. There is still a lot to be learned when sitting mat side.

It is crucial for your recovery that you do not aggravate any current injuries. Protect your injury at all times. This may require you to take a hand, arm, leg, or foot out of the equation when trying to establish grips and hooks. Training with a temporary disability can be beneficial in presenting opportunity to develop other aspects of your jiu-jitsu game.

It is important to always check first with your physician and BJJ instructor to assess your ability to train when injured before stepping back on the mats.

Strength Supplements

Whey protein:

This is a fast absorbing protein. For this reason, it is a great protein for pre and post training. I would at least use this protein after your training session to assist in the muscle recovery process.

Caseinate:

This protein is slow digesting. Casein gives you a constant flow of protein, because of the time it takes the body to break down. For this reason, this protein is used before bed to counter the period of fasting your body goes through when at rest.

Soy protein:

This is a midrange protein. This protein fits between fast digesting whey and slow digesting casein protein.

Creatine:

Creatine is effective at increasing muscle and strength. It also increases muscle performance in athletes.

Joint Supplements

Cissus (Cissus Quadrangularis):

In my experience, this herbal supplement has been most effective at alleviating any joint soreness/pain. Most joint supplements take a while to build up in your system before even getting marginal results. Cissus usually only takes about a day, or two to notice substantial results.

Glucosamine and Chondroitin:

This combo is one of the better known joint supplements. Some experience good results with this, but must follow a strict regimen of supplementation over a period of time to achieve any results.

Omega-3:

This is a great supplement for overall health that is also good for alleviating joint pain due to its anti-inflammatory properties.

Turmeric Curcumin:

There are a number of health benefits in addition to the anti-inflammatory properties of turmeric curcumin.

Boron:

Boron is a vital trace mineral that has great joint benefits. This supplement is effective at alleviating many joint issues.

The Blue Belt Relationship Counselor

As with white belts, blue belts have the highest dropout rate in Brazilian jiu-jitsu. Let's look at what some of the factors there are that contribute to this problem and some of the solutions.

Note: *The information in this section applies to all levels of BJJ practitioners in handling potential obstacles that may negatively impact training.*

Life getting in the way:

I can understand how the business and constant motion of life can potentially get in the way of jiu-jitsu training. I have a full time job in addition to being married with five beautiful children that I actively care for.

The solution to this problem is to organize your time, and set priorities. Even with a busy life and schedule, it is possible to organize your time in a way to make the most out of your day. If you limit the less productive activities in your day, and prioritize the important things, you will begin to find the necessary time to facilitate progress in relationships, career, and BJJ.

Stagnant in Progress:

It is at this level of blue belt in your training that you may run into the majority of plateaus.

It isn't realistic to expect that there won't be challenges, or obstacles to overcome in any good relationship. It is when you make it through those tough times (plateaus/walls) that will be most rewarding. Review the section Plateaus/Walls in this book to help you overcome these obstacles.

Complacency:

This could be due to the longer stretch it typically takes for one to go from blue belt to purple. When the average blue belt takes about three years to reach the next belt promotion, it may create a complacent attitude for those who measure all their achievements and success on just the color of their belt. This mindset is a way to set yourself up for failure.

Setting goals in specific areas of your training is the best route to overcoming complacency. With this, give concentrated focus on key areas that could benefit your overall game. A possible goal could be, getting better at passing the De La Riva guard. Now take a couple weeks to implement a game plan to achieve your goal with focused drilling and rolling. As you make improvement, enjoy the little successes in your training.

General Frustration:

There are areas of frustration in BJJ that may contribute to the dropout rate. After all, jiu-jitsu is an activity that greatly challenges the mind, body, pride, patience, etc.

There will be many times where you show up to class hoping to dominate, but instead you get smashed all over the mats. If you don't have the right mindset to humbly take this as a learning opportunity, pride will negatively affect your heart for jiu-jitsu.

Remember, that even at higher levels of jiu-jitsu, there is always going to be training partners, or competitors that could get the better of you in this ever evolving sport. The better you get at jiu-jitsu, the more important it may be to maintain a humble attitude.

Injury can also play a discouraging role in your connection with the sport. This can stall your training for extended periods of time.

Review the Injury section of this book to limit the frequency of these events, and use this time effectively.

Rekindle:

Here are some points of advice to help you rekindle your relationship with BJJ. The first is to remember why you fell in love with jiu-jitsu in the first place. There is probably a list of reasons why you started training, along with all the time you have invested in BJJ already. This may include, but is not limited to the following:

- Increased fitness level (look and feel your best)

- Competition

- Challenges the Body and Mind

- Ability to Protect Yourself (self-defense)

- Builds Confidence

- Relieve Stress

- Social Aspect (all the friends made within the jiu-jitsu community)

If you focus on the positives, and work through the negatives, your relationship setbacks will only be temporary. You have to ask yourself if this relationship is worth fighting for, and if it is, pull guard.

Made in the USA
Middletown, DE
08 February 2022

59963196R00066